CELEBRATING THE CITY OF ABU DHABI

Celebrating the City of Abu Dhabi

Walter the Educator

Silent King Books

Copyright © 2024 by Walter the Educator

All rights reserved. No part of this book may be reproduced in any manner whatsoever without written per- mission except in the case of brief quotations embodied in critical articles and reviews.

First Printing, 2024

Disclaimer

This book is a literary work; the story is not about specific persons, locations, situations, and/or circumstances unless mentioned in a historical context. Any resemblance to real persons, locations, situations, and/or circumstances is coincidental. This book is for entertainment and informational purposes only. The author and publisher offer this information without warranties expressed or implied. No matter the grounds, neither the author nor the publisher will be accountable for any losses, injuries, or other damages caused by the reader's use of this book. The use of this book acknowledges an understanding and acceptance of this disclaimer.

Celebrating the City of Abu Dhabi is a little collectible souvenir book that belongs to the Celebrating Cities Book Series by Walter the Educator. Collect them all and more books at WaltertheEducator.com

USE THE EXTRA SPACE TO TAKE NOTES AND DOCUMENT YOUR MEMORIES

ABU DHABI

In the heart of desert sands, where whispers find their grace,

Celebrating the City of Abu Dhab

Lies Abu Dhabi, an oasis, where the sun bestows its face.

Skyscrapers pierce the azure sky, like sentinels of light,

Guardians of a legacy, resplendent in the night.

Beneath the palm's green canopy, the dates of time unfold,

Histories are woven, like the tapestries of old.

From the sands of Liwa's crescent, to the shores of Corniche's shore,

Abu Dhabi whispers stories, of a past that's evermore.

Golden domes of grandeur, reflect the dawn's first ray,

Sheikh Zayed's white marbles, where believers kneel and pray.

An emblem of serenity, its minarets so high,

Calling souls to harmony, beneath the azure sky.

A dance of modern marvels, with roots in ancient lore,

A symphony of contrasts, where past and future soar.

In souks where spices mingle, with the scent of oud and rose,

Tradition's heartbeats linger, in every breeze that blows.

Celebrating the City of Abu Dhab

The falcon's flight soars noble, through a realm of endless blue,

An emblem of the spirit, proud and ever true.

From the mangroves' emerald whisper, to the dunes' golden crest,

Nature weaves her magic, in this land so blessed.

Pearls from ocean's deep embrace, once traded, now revered,

Echo tales of divers bold, whose courage never feared.

Each shell a silent chronicle, of waters crystal clear,

Where dreams were forged in depths, beyond the reach of fear.

On Saadiyat's bright beaches, where the art of worlds converge,

Museums rise like beacons, where cultures find their surge.

Louvre's wings outstretched, invite the curious mind,

To journey through the epochs, where art and heart entwined.

Yas Marina's circuit winds, with engines' thrilling roar,

Echoes of ambition, as speeds and spirits soar.

A realm of endless ventures, from heights to ocean's floor,

Celebrating the City of
Abu Dhab

Where dreams are penned in starlight, and hopes forevermore.

In gardens where the fountains, with their whispered secrets play,

Children's laughter echoes, like the dawn's first golden ray.

A city's pulse is vibrant, with each footstep on its way,

A tapestry of stories, in the heat of the midday.
Celebrating the City of Abu Dhab

Cultural Foundation's whispers, in halls of timeless grace,

Pages of the poets, find their voice, their place.

A testament to knowledge, where wisdom finds its home,

In the heart of Abu Dhabi, where thoughts and dreams roam.

ABOUT THE CREATOR

Walter the Educator is one of the pseudonyms for Walter Anderson. Formally educated in Chemistry, Business, and Education, he is an educator, an author, a diverse entrepreneur, and he is the son of a disabled war veteran. "Walter the Educator" shares his time between educating and creating. He holds interests and owns several creative projects that entertain, enlighten, enhance, and educate, hoping to inspire and motivate you. Follow, find new works, and stay up to date with Walter the Educator™

at WaltertheEducator.com

www.ingramcontent.com/pod-product-compliance
Lightning Source LLC
LaVergne TN
LVHW052007060526
838201LV00059B/3891